Passive Income for the Average Joe

18 Methods to Generate over $10,000 a Month and Become Financially Free in a Few Weeks

by Trevis White

The following Book is reproduced below with the goal of providing information that is as accurate and reliable as possible. Regardless, purchasing this Book can be seen as consent to the fact that both the publisher and the author of this book are in no way experts on the topics discussed within and that any recommendations or suggestions that are made herein are for entertainment purposes only. Professionals should be consulted as needed prior to undertaking any of the action endorsed herein.

This declaration is deemed fair and valid by both the American Bar Association and the Committee of Publishers Association and is legally binding throughout the United States.

Furthermore, the transmission, duplication, or reproduction of any of the following work including specific information will be considered an illegal act irrespective of if it is done electronically or in print. This extends to creating a secondary or tertiary copy of the work or a recorded copy and is only allowed with express written consent from the Publisher. All additional rights reserved.

The information in the following pages is broadly considered to be a truthful and accurate account of facts and as such any inattention, use or misuse of the information in question by the reader will render any resulting actions solely under their purview. There are no scenarios in which the publisher or the original author of this work can be in any fashion deemed liable for any hardship or damages that may befall them after undertaking information described herein.

Additionally, the information in the following pages is intended only for informational purposes and should thus be thought of as universal. As befitting its nature, it is presented without assurance regarding its prolonged validity or interim quality. Trademarks that are mentioned are done without written consent and can in no way be considered an endorsement from the trademark holder.

Table of Contents

About the author

My name is Trevis White and I am a professional trader and investor. I have always wanted to understand the language of money and to grasp the tactics that rich people use to accumulate wealth. At first, I thought that they were just lucky. However, after reading "Rich Dad Poor Dad" by Robert Kiyosaki, I was forced to change my mind. There is a reason why riches keep getting richer and poor people tend to stay broke for their entire life. I dedicated my life to finding this reason and to share it with others.

After attending seminars all over the world, a friend of mine asked "Alvin why don't you write a book about it? I really think other people could benefit from what you know". At first, I was a bit sceptical. I mean, why should others seek advice from me, when there are hundreds of other gurus around? However, after reasoning on it for a while, I came to the conclusion that I had something different: I actually did invest myself. You see, it is so easy to find books and videos by authors that claim to have made millions of dollars, as if it was the simplest thing in the world. I do not even try to claim to have earned so much money. I mean, do not get me wrong, I have made several hundred thousands dollars in my life, but I have yet to come close to the two comma club. Why am I saying this to you? Because I believe in honesty and building trust. After all, I have started writing book as a hobby and I do not need my customers' money to survive. This is what gave me the confidence to stand up and speak my truth: I hope you appreciate it.

Enough of me, now. It is time to get down to business and start learning!

Introduction

Congratulations on downloading *Passive Income: 18 Strategies to Make 12,487$ a Month and Become Financially Free* and thank you for doing so.

The following chapters will discuss what passive income is and how you can get the most out of time by doing high value money activities. When it comes to creating a passive income stream, there are a lot of things to consider and this book wants to get into details about every aspect needed to take conscious and smart investing decisions.

This book will provide you with 18 amazing strategies, that have allowed me to make 12,487$ a month and become financially free. Not only that, though. It will also give you a complete overview of the most famous concept that every online marketer should learn: how to properly delegate activities to make the most money.

The goal of the book is to speed up your education and save you time and money along the way.

Before getting started, it is important to note something about mindset. This, as the other books in the series, do not offer "get rich quick solutions", since they do not exists. Especially when you are beginning your journey in creating an online business, it is fundamental to focus on learning and acquiring new information, rather than just chasing money. With the right knowledge, results will come much faster and you will be amazed by what you can accomplish, even with a small capital. The book wants to give you the tools you need to get started and share with you some of the golden nuggets that made other people wealthy. If you study this material carefully and start applying it, you will lay out the foundation for prosperity and wealth.

There are plenty of books on this subject on the market, thanks again for choosing this one! Every effort was made to ensure it is full of as much useful information as possible, please enjoy!

Chapter 1

7 Important notes on the right mindset to achieve passive income

Before getting started, it is very important to understand something about mindset. In fact, most people that are chasing passive income, try to get it with a passive mentality. This is the worst mistake that can be made, since it is the straightest road to failure. If you want to create a business that goes on autopilot, it is important to be proactive and take life by the horns. Here are 7 tips that it are important to understand, before getting started.

1. 'Passive income' is a viral idea

It is as viral as the idea that you can be doing what you love the most and in the meantime making a lot of money. To the bank clerk, to the newsagent, to the entrepreneur who hustles all day having to do with clients, this idea seems like a dream. Drop everything - and devote yourself to what you like to do - and let the money arrive on your account by itself. If it was not such a viral idea it would not be possible to explain why it is enough for a person to attend two or three courses of personal development to be automatically 'subscribed' to the idea of passive income.

2.   Is it possible to create passive streams of income?

Yes, in my opinion as long as you work hard for 4 or 5 years to learn your specific area of expertise, how to organize work in a certain way and how to monetize your clients the most, it is definitely possible. The point to understand here is that it takes a lot of time and perseverance. And no, one month is not a lot of time.

3.   Ok, I understand: you want to leave a job that you do not like, create passive income and dedicate yourself to the one you love the most.

But then excuse me, since you have to spend 4 or 5 years to study how to create passive income and then dedicate yourself to what you love, why do you not spend that time trying to figure out how to turn what you love most in a job?

What I advise you to do is: do what you want, and turn it into a job. It takes a certain character to do it, and we must also know how to do it. Among other things, it is one of the ideas you will hear the most about in the self development niche.

4. **The 'pure' passive income does not exist.** Unless you make a great marriage, or win the lottery - even managing the system that gives you money 'automatically' takes time and effort. I have friends who do network marketing. With this idea of creating their passive income they have more meetings than the CEO of Burger King, they meet a lot of potential customers to create their own network. And you want to tell me that it is not work? And do you think that the network should not be kept adjured and nourished, after it is created?

5. Choose something that you like so much that you do not even think about it as a job. This will greatly facilitate the creation of a true passive income.

I know people who wanted to create their passive income by doing stock trading (one of the thing I am an expert in – I have written multiple books about this topic). They are the most stressed people I know in the world, by dint of being behind systems, numbers and everything else that work entails. Would you be able to manage it?

When will you have your passive income (you decide how much) what do you want to dedicate yourself to? It's worth spending some time trying to answer this question - Probably the key to your professional evolution is here. It's something that people never think about. They spend their lives thinking that first they have to do something that cares of the money and then dedicate themselves to something they really love to do. From a logical point of view it is a nonsense. Yet choosing what you love and trying to make it the centre of your work seems to be the hardest thing in the world.

6. Creating a passive income is always a 'process' not an ending act, and to follow this process you must learn to anticipate the change that takes place in the system.

Years ago one of the most effective systems to generate 'almost passive' income was to open an automatic videotape rental business, just to say. Today there are no more automatic videotape rental stores and I have not seen one for at least 10 years. How many systems that today are able to generate a passive income are able to sustain this capacity over time? This is an important question to ask yourself, if you want to be in this game for the long term.

7. Creating 'passive income' is possible only if you are willing to change your mindset and the way you operate.

The way you decide to organize yourself, your job, and that of your, collaborators to bring the whole system into a position where it has a very strong sense of identity - and operates from there. When all the people in the organization align 'who they are' to what they do - the whole structure becomes more efficient by several orders of magnitude. And only then, in my opinion, it is possible to start thinking about generating passive income.

Chapter 2

An introduction to passive income

Hands up those who have never dreamed, even if only for a moment, about a life based on economic independence and financial freedom, where there was no need to work because the money comes from passive income streams of some kind, which eventually require only a monitoring and some occasional 'adjustment' to keep them alive.

In order to live on passive income, however, it is necessary to have available a starting capital which, invested in an intelligent manner, is able to produce precisely the income that is necessary for you to live and which can also cope with the process of inflation, that as you know is not controllable by individuals.

I will not spend words to explain how much money you need to live on passive income, nor will I give advice on investment methods or real estate, since they are not my responsibility, but I will try to advise you some sources of passive income that will allow you to create an online automatic income that does not require special investments if not your intelligence, your experience and your time.

Of course, stop here and do not continue reading if you are not willing to make any effort to find that famous balance between income and expenses mentioned earlier, and if it makes you sick if you commit to a project that will only allow you to earn 50 or 100 euro per month online (one of many, of course, because it is a replicable mechanism, as we will see shortly).

I do not know how many of you like to travel and visit new places, personally as a digital nomad as I am, the possibility of going to Spain, England and the rest of the world by continuing to manage my online activities from anywhere in the world is an aspect that I feel is particularly fascinating.

Of course it is not something that I have always done, even though for most of my first fifty years of life I have worked mainly as a freelancer, so independently and being able to manage in full freedom the rhythms and working time (provided you deliver work on time, of course). But for some time I have also worked as a 'subordinate', commuting or working at night, enduring the uprisings in the middle of winter and uncomfortable train journeys, taking on extraordinary and exhausting shifts and everything that employee life can offer to those who he is forced to live it. All this, or having experienced the two sides of the coin, convinced me to do everything (including some sacrifice) just to conquer and keep the freedom deriving from freelance work and a passive income lifestyle.

The real breakthrough, however, was that of passive income, derived mainly from working on the Web and at online projects.

But what is passive income? In general, it is considered money earned without moving a finger or even while sleeping (it is not an exaggeration, as you will see shortly). Beware, however, because the so-called passive income is never completely passive, or at least not risky if you do not, at least sometimes, do something to 'support' the sources from which the streams derive. In fact, while doing so you have the opportunity to feed the sources of passive income and to grow them.

However, it is right to immediately clarify a fundamental point, and underline again what was said at the beginning of this chapter: to create passive income without necessarily investing money you can rely only on your intelligence, your tenacity, your experience (the famous know -how) and on your time. You must therefore have all these resources available and use them together to create a model of automatic and passive income on the Internet.

In addition, you will have to work towards specific objectives and focusing on them, avoiding to disperse yourself in a thousand things and focusing only on what really matters to achieve the results you have set. In short, you will have to apply the famous 80/20 rule. What is it? Let's see in the next chapter.

Chapter 3

The 80/20 Rule

O k, just a short history lesson - come on, do not sit there staring at the emptiness. Have you ever heard of the 80/20 rule? Someti- mes they call it the principle of the scarcity of factors, and it was originally called the Pareto Principle. It was born at the beginning of the 20th century, when Vilfre- do Pareto discovered that in Italy 80 percent of the land was owned by 20 percent of the population.

Fast forward a few years, we realized how the rule could be applied in the business world. In most cases, 20 percent of the customers represent the vast majority, or 80 percent, of their turnover. And today the 80/20 rule lends itself to any kind of interesting interpretation.

To take advantage of the 80/20 rule within your company, you focus on 20 percent of the best customers, which guarantee you 80 percent of your sales.

To take advantage of the 80/20 rule to manage your time you focus on 20 percent of the things you do, the ones that matter to you or your business. In other words, the highest value activities (also called "high money value activities").

Pareto's law is dramatically effective when applied to sales and marketing situations. However, the use of Pareto's theory in sales and marketing is generally neglected completely.

The Pareto rule at the simple level suggests that, if there are two groups of data typically related to cause and effect, or input and output, the correlation measured by the data of reality is that:

> "80 percent of the output is produced by 20 percent of the inputs"

"80 percent of the results are given by 20 percent of the causes"

"20% of the nature of the costs generates 80% in absolute value of the costs"

"20% of customers generate 80% of revenues"
"20% of products generate 80% of revenues"
"20% of non-compliance causes 80% of non-compliance

You can apply this relationship to any kind of variable. The Pareto principle is an extremely useful model or theory, with infinite applications. Often the optimal ratio in terms of identifying the minimum percentage that will produce the best improvement is closer to 90:10 or even 99: 1.

The numbers in their ratio must not necessarily reach 100. The two numbers in an optimal ratio can have more than 100 or less than 100.

For example, there may be a situation where 99% of the result is produced by 15% of the factors or when 75% of the results are derived from 5% of the factors. So even if a situation contains an 80:20 correlation, other relationships may be more significant, for example:

99:22 (which demonstrates an even greater concentration of 80:20)

5:50 (ie 5% of the results comes from 50% of inputs or causes) which means a huge amount of activities with ineffective content).

The reasons that allowed the 80:20 ratio to become the "standard" relationship is that on large numbers it remains the most surprising and commonly found relationship in reality.

Remember, for any particular situation the precise ratio can and will probably be different from 80:20, but the principle still applies and in many cases the actual ratio will not be far from the general rule of 80:20.

This principle is extremely useful for planning, analysing and solving problems and achieving goals.

Many disasters in the business could have been easily avoided with a consistent approach of the Pareto Principle. It is a tremendously powerful model, and it is so powerful because it is so simple and easy.

For example, consider an organization that continues to run its business across its product range, when perhaps 95% of its profits come from just 10% of the products and / or perhaps only 2% of its profits comes from 60%, the same with reference to customers.

Imagine the wasted effort. Instead, by making a quick analysis of "Pareto's rule" by discovering this reality, decision makers can clearly see where to direct their efforts, and probably reduce a lot of bad products and better focus on customers and products that are more profitable.

4 Ways to achieve passive income

But let's see what the main ways to create a passive and automatic monthly online income are:

1. Sell one or more services, automating the process as much as possible.

2. Sell content, in the form of books, ebooks, courses or info-products.

3. Selling through others, earning from affiliation.

4. Monetize content published in other ways (eg with advertising space)

At the moment I (like many others here in America and in the rest of the world) earn from all 4 sources. Naturally, each of these ways of creating passive income presupposes the initial work and, in many cases, also the subsequent work although sporadic to maintain the vitality of the source of income. As you have noticed, in fact, in all three cases we talk about "selling", which presupposes that there are buyers and that there is a need to reach them by letting them know in some way (possibly without investing in advertising), and at the same time that there is a "product" to sell to these people, something that may interest them for any reason.

We will try to examine this four ways one by one, so that you can understand which one is the best one for you, that is, with which you feel more affinity in relation to your interests, your passions and your abilities.

1. Passive income from the sale of services or online applications

This is one of the most effective methods to create an automated passive online income, but unlike the other three methods presented below it requires a small investment to register a suitable domain and Web space, as well as greater technical expertise.

For this type of passive income, in fact, we consider services such as ad sites or those that allow you to manage technical aspects of activity on the Web, proposed in the freemium formula, or with a free basic version that involves limitations of use and a more complete paid version where the limitations are 'unlocked'.

In the first category there are, for example, sites where people can post ads of various kinds made with themes or dedicated plugins (using CMS as WordPress), such as those for the sale of used equipment or to meet other people (ad sites) or online dating, or tourist portals that give visibility to advertisers and earn every time they sell their service (it is the case of the hospitality industry with sites like TripAdvisor, Wimdu, etc.), or other sites that put freelancers with potential customers in connection, and so on.

In the second category, on the other hand, there may be included sites that manage, for example, the backup of a site or its maintenance, facilitate networking or collaborative activities of a professional nature, and so on. It goes without saying that it is not enough to develop and put online this type of services, but that we must then promote them both initially and periodically so that more and more people are registered, and naturally we must manage them with an equally regular maintenance to avoid problems of stability or security on the site that provides them.

In addition to the sites there may also be true applications, both in the form of computer software (desktop PC) and mobile devices (smartphones and tablets) in the form of an app. In this case the skills required for their development are even greater, and once again there will be a need for promotion to make them known and updated over time to correct any stability and security bugs or improve their functionality making them even more attractive. Of this second sector are, of course, also the games, often proposed with a freemium formula and distributed as an app or inserted into websites (eg in gambling or multi-user games) or on social networks. Probably those who read will have already had the opportunity to play some of these games, or to take advantage of some services like those listed above.

At this point it will be clearer what we mean when we say that there is no totally passive income, a concept that we will find even later, and it is therefore important to underline.

2. **Passive income from the sale of contents**
When we talk about content we refer not only to those that form an ebook or a book, but also to images that a photographer can sell on sites specialized in stock images, or to video and to the audio sold in the same way. In all these cases, passive income streams will derive from the repeated sale of each individual content, which may produce a proper revenue if it is conducted on its own or partial if sold through a distribution platform. The latter are represented, for example, by traditional book stores or those online in the case of books and ebooks, from the already mentioned sites that sell images (photos and

drawings), video or audio for professional purposes such as the development of sites or multimedia products, or again from sites that host, for example, online courses if the contents already mentioned represent, for example, a video course or an audio course.

In all these cases, the content must be produced only once and then placed on the market through an automated sales system, and this is how the flow of passive income is created resulting from its sale. As can be understood, even for content, promotion and marketing are essential if we want to increase sales rather than simply wait for someone to notice them and buy them (something that happens), and for those contents that are subject to obsolescence (for for example, courses on technical subjects) it is also necessary to proceed with periodic updates so that they remain attractive to the public and do not become too old (and therefore no longer valid) because someone decides to buy them again.

A strategy often used by those who live from the production of content is to offer a part (or a 'fragmented' version) for free, for example through a site or a blog, and create parallel commercial versions that collect them as a book / ebook, full course, and so on. In this way it becomes possible to create a 'showcase' able to support the commercially distributed 'works', and thus increase sales.

3. Passive income from affiliate marketing

If you do not want to sell your services, products or content, you can always do it with those of others by earning a percentage of those sales and thus creating another form of passive income. In this case, however, the sale takes place outside of your site, directly on that of the seller. In America, the opportunities for affiliation are many and offer ample earning space.

Passive affiliate streams of income can also derive from sources other than a website, for example from content published on social networks, but in this case they have a shorter duration in time as they go into the background as time passes and it becomes less likely that the public will notice them and click on the respective links (unless you periodically invest in paid visibility, as you do for example on Facebook, highlighting the payment of a post, but in this case we will fall into passive generated by a cash investment, however minimal, so it is not appropriate to include it in this chapter. Do not worry, we will talk about passive streams of income that require a money investment in the next chapter.

4. Passive returns from other monetization of contents

The latter category may include, for example, services such as the sale, or rather the rental of advertising space on a site or app that enjoys a certain popularity / visibility. The advertising spaces can be represented by text in a directory, by banners or entire pages, as happens for example in the sites / portals that are positioned in the tourism sector and rent a space to managers of hotel, restaurant and similar activities inside of strategic areas of the site. What has just been said at the end of the previous paragraph is more valid than ever in such a field, given that advertisers will be more likely to pay their periodic share the more they are certain of gaining visibility through the site.

The same applies to the app, once they have achieved the necessary popularity, but the latter typically require investments in marketing and advertising to gain visibility among the public.

This type of passive income should not be confused with income generated through systems such as those used by portals like TripAdvisor, obviously, as in this case it is an automated service and therefore falls into the first type of online passive income described in this chapter.

Chapter 5

14 Strategies to create passive income

Now that we have laid out the foundation and seen the four ways make passive income possible, it is time to get our hands dirty. In fact, theory it is not enough: strategies are fundamental. Here you will find 14 proven methods that have allowed me to generate more than 12,487$ a month and become financially free.

1. Sell an Ebook

The model much loved by bloggers and those who start to promote themselves online all over the world and for good reason. It is quite easy to write a 60-80 page ebook, and it is not difficult to sell 500 copies a month through online networking, Affiliate publication and your own SEO optimized blog.

The thing to watch out for is the price. Pay attention to the niches where the public is just willing to pay 5 euros for an ebook; It's always a good idea to repackage your ebook so you can sell it on Amazon (as a Kindle-only version) and iBooks, since many people will also be looking for it there.

If you add this feature, make sure you have a price lower than 10 euros on these sites, as this seems to be the maximum price for these audiences and allows you to get a higher percentage for Amazon and Apple payout rules.

Oh, do not worry, people who buy your ebook through these platform, 9 times out of 10 would not buy it otherwise, so you are not losing money by listing your book on third party sites.

But if you really want to make money with an ebook, then you have to create a list of emails or rely on a list of affiliates who join you for sale.

Whether you contact affiliates one by one, and / or start putting your products on affiliate marketplaces like Clickbank, the secret is simply to connect with as many people as possible, giving them all the tools they need to sell your ebook.

As an alternative to ClickBank also evaluates Gumroad, is one of the best platforms used for the sale of digital products such as E-Books, audio, video, SAAS and much more.

Gumroad also has a very lean and easy to use affiliate program.

2. Create a Blog

It's even easier to make money this way than with an ebook, because all you need to do is to focus on your site's content and get traffic - most of the people who engage in this online business can get an affiliate sale within 30 days of starting a blog.

But above all, now you can earn from the sale of all types of products; information products (info-products) of your property and made by others, online tools and resources, physical products, books, etc.!

Depending on which niche you choose, affiliate commissions can vary widely.

It is better to promote products in niches where most creators have already set up affiliate programs; For example, the small business support niche all have affiliate programs, from hosting providers, to WordPress theme creators, to online course teachers.

On the contrary, promoting fitness equipment can be much more difficult as most providers do not have affiliate programs set up and ready for registration, or at least not configured in a very intuitive way.

To be really successful with affiliate marketing, it is very important that your blog / website focuses on a specific niche and that you only sharpen it for products in that area of interest (eg, juicer machines, luxury watches, household supplies, ebooks etc.), because your readers will trust your opinion and therefore will be convinced enough to be ready to buy from you.

The best products with which to make an Affiliate Blog include digital products such as ebooks or online courses (you get super high percentages, often 50% and above) and recurring online services (if they offer continuous reference rates, such as hosting, hazard, etc.).

Another small piece of advice that I would like to give you with affiliate marketing is to replace many of your affiliate links on your website and link to free stuff like free ebooks, courses for starters, e-mails, etc. Not only does this help your site look less "spammy" in the eyes of Google, but visitors are much more likely to click on links into useful free resources they enjoy / trust (and do not feel like they are forced to buy).

3. Sell An Online Course With Membership

I'm talking about a multimedia website reserved for paying members. So, unlike other passive income ideas, such as blog + adsense, here you can really open up to the idea of making money by teaching people something super specific, for example how to breed hunting dogs!

We speak of sites with restricted access where people pay to consult or download content (video lessons, tutorials, eBooks, podcasts etc.) and digital products (plugins, templates, MP3 files, MP4 etc.). We are therefore in the context of the info-products sold through a membership site. With a membership you can create online returns over time simply by recording a series of lessons, uploading them to your site and making them available only to paying users, maybe gradually, like 4 lessons a week for 6 months.

4. Create a Comparison Products Site

Here is how it works: you have to find a niche in which there are a ton of products, all with a lot of semi-complex functionality - or just about any kind of niche where customers are going to choose a product but who have not the slightest idea what to buy.

Now create a site that firstly shares a series of useful content (think tutorials, how to do for etc) on the niche in question and secondly review each product / service in that niche through a mix of text, photos and video reviews.

Furthermore, it creates a comparison table page in which each product is listed and evaluated on a series of functions, all side by side. The customer can finally decide which product is right for him through this table with a quick look, in addition to the detailed articles / videos of individual reviews. Next to each product there is a link to the seller's purchase page (eg Amazon), and you guessed it, those links are affiliate links.

5. Open An E-Commerce Store

This idea is for those who have decided to do some serious online marketing with automatic income. There is a lot of work at the beginning and compared to other ideas, you have to consider a lot of work on an ongoing basis. But if you automate this business as much as possible, you can reduce it to a few hours a week.

Anyway, here is the idea. Find a product or group where there is a lot of demand (for example, accessories or food for dogs / cats, car accessories, etc.), and then create your online store.

Sign a drop-shipping agreement directly with a reliable supplier and voila!

But returning to the main thing here; look for products that are as small as possible and cost between € 50 and € 200, they are inexpensive to ship, are rather stable over time (ie they are not always updated / modified / sold out) and can not be easily purchased online (eg cameras digital devices are easy to buy, while something like furniture, beds or mattresses are much more difficult).

6. Selling Advertising Space

I am not talking about writing a blog about cats and inserting a bit of Google Adsense in there.

I am talking about setting up an all-in-one guide-style website for a specific niche (such as a travel blog for people moving abroad, or more specifically on the best hotels for families staying in the Canaries, or a beginner's guide to SUV cars on the market) and then actively going out to find companies that may want to buy direct advertising space on your site once you get X number of highly qualified (and high-value) readers.

Now, very importantly, when I say "advertising" I want you to think a bit out of the box.

This is not just banner advertising - in fact, traditional banner ads are disgusting as a conversion, or invite people to click to reach the advertiser.

Much more intelligent direct advertising methods could include the sale of spaces for guest posts (ie the advertiser writes a useful article for your target market and then links it to their products and how it can help solve the problem x), or sell text links within your information-rich articles (these have impressive click through rates).

The example that comes to mind is a travel blog. Here you can have an Expedia booking widget and a travel insurance widget in the sidebar where normally there would be a simple display ad.

The beauty is that visitors can begin to "buy" directly from the sidebar of the site of travel bloggers, with the transaction that then proceeds to the site of advertisers when required. The involvement factor of interactive widgets is beautiful and, as a result, can generate much higher click-through rates.

If you set up 10 content-rich static driving websites, you could earn an attractive income in 12 months!

7. Build An Online Store For A Real Service and Outsource the Work

That is why it is easier if I give you an example that I am thinking about launching soon.

Build and optimize SEO website for people trying to convert 8mm-VHS videos to DVD / USB.

Make the website very easy to use, so that the user has no way to ask questions, everything is clear right away.

And he can then send his order online and pay directly via PayPal.

Be sure to evaluate your service with an award as this will help you get a good profit after paying the outsourced work, but I have no doubt that if you have a clean, reliable, easy to use and navigate site, you can request a prize (just like in real-world stores).

Now make sure you have a clear and simple order form clearly visible on the website with a reliable payment gateway configuration.

After the customer has completed the process, the payment is sent to you and then all the details entered in the order form are automatically sent to your VHS-DVD video outsourcing converter that you have chosen.

After payment, the customer is redirected to a page that contains all the details he needs later; where to publish their videos, when to wait for them, etc. Once again we are working hard now, to make sure there is no confusion, no questions and no need for customer support on an ongoing basis.

Your trusted shop with which you collaborate gets the videos, performs the conversion and sends them to the customer. You confirm with the customer that he is satisfied and only then pay the supplier his share. Done.

Do not touch anything and only once a week or even a month, you have to settle with the store.

Think of how many service companies in the real world you could use to o this process: scan photos, print business cards, etc.

8. Create an app for IPhone or IPad

Creating an app is not as expensive as you think. And if you want to create an application based primarily on information, there are a lot of easy-to-use online do-it-yourself programs for a couple of hundred euros.

I'm not a big fan of this idea. But I think if you can put your App in the App Store you may win the "lottery".

9. Create Your YouTube Channel

Well, I think getting traffic on a blog is much more difficult than getting views on You Tube these days, because the world of text content is so frighteningly full (and therefore very competitive), while the video world is so relatively empty since many people are too shy to turn their knowledge into video.
On the other hand, people prefer to watch more than 10 videos that read 1-2 blog posts, as the average attention (which means more possibilities to get clicks with the video) is much higher when listening to a video than when reading a post.

It is well known that Google prefers You Tube in their search results significantly, often by entering videos for the search term at the top or top of the page, without ever really knowing the quality of the video, apart from the title, description and the tags.

And yes, You Tube is the second largest search engine in the world.

But the thing that really makes me think that this is a solid passive earning opportunity is the time to reward your work; For example, creating a YouTube video on a topic takes 5 minutes, literally, while writing the equivalent may take an hour longer.

What really helps with You Tube is if you choose a technical topic to record videos on; the type of topic in which someone is trying to solve a problem. So when they watch your video and see a relevant ad for a perfect product for them, they are more likely to click.

You can monetize a video by clicking on the "Monetization" tab and checking the "Monetize with ads" box. To monetize a video after it has been uploaded, open "Video Manager" and click on the euro symbol "€" next to the video. Check the "monetize with ads" box.

The more clicks will receive the more YouTube will send you advertising revenue.

Compare this configuration with a comic or generalist vlogger. They may get more views, but there is little chance that the same relevance of the ad and the same combination of snack products for viewers.

10. Create Software or a Simple Online Application

Whatever it is, from WordPress themes to online productivity tools to a specific industry thing like an online billing service for architects, this could make you rich and generate automatic revenue for a long time.

What if I was not a programmer? Well simple, you can get all the heavy work done by outsourcing professionals, and then deal with the online software sales alone through marketing techniques.

A long time ago there has been discussions on what is best: info products vs software, to make money online (passive or not). I must say that being a reseller of information against a software vendor is really a personal thing.

Both have their pros and cons, and after analysing them deeply I can not give you a definitive response.

One thing I will say is that if you have little or no technical skills / background, go for a software product as your first attempt to create a passive income stream is risky. You could find yourself from the beginning with a cost of 10,000 euros for the design before even having a product ready to go on the market.

But really underline how easy it is to make money with a software; for example, creating a PowerPoint graphics package that people can use to quickly create app prototypes and other templates (this is actually an idea that someone had, checkout Keynotopia, which makes the creator about $ 8,000 a month according to the his recent presentation).

Or do a simple niche WordPress theme (or get it done by a programmer on Up-work). With just 1000 euros of investment you have a pretty good source of income for the next few years.

11. Create A Book Review Website

Let's talk about site 1 in the world where to buy books. Amazon, with thousands of titles to choose from: bestsellers, new releases, offers, children's books, thrillers, thrillers, cooking, fiction, Amazon Original Books, biographies, comics, football and much more. Obviously your monetization strategy here is Amazon's affiliate link. Create a review site and link the book cover with the Amazon affiliate link and it's done.

12. Create A 'Fake' Store And Connect It To

Amazon

This is different from the idea of e-commerce, because here it is not an online store you are building, but rather a site full of content with tons of articles and videos focused on the product.

That is to say one idea is for an online store and the other for a blog / affiliate site of sorts.

The important points to follow here are to index on search engines a site in a niche of physical products, where you talk about specific products, so that the people who arrive on your site are pre-qualified, ie they are people who are already doing research on a specific product and are ready to buy as soon as they find a site that provides that product.

All you need to do is get people to click on your Amazon affiliate link. That is all.

Once they get to Amazon, they can purchase the product (you get paid a commission although your Amazon affiliate cookie expires within 24 hours of the person clicking).

You can resort to a trick, the EasyAzon plugin, that will allow you to increase the duration of Amazon cookies for up to 90 days!

Many users unfortunately do not buy immediately, but after one or more days: as a result, the affiliate will lose all the commissions of the people who will buy at a later time on Amazon (although having clicked on our link).

To increase the profits, therefore, we must resort to this trick that allows you to extend the duration of cookies. If the product is placed in the cart the cookie will last for 90 days. This is definitely better, right?

Your article can summarize all the different products for a particular use, review them or compare them to similar ones. We do not care about keeping people on our site, we actually want them to go to Amazon, so make everything clickable, including images of affiliate-encoded products, purchase buttons, etc.

Another piece of advice, is to enter the affiliation of both high-cost and low-cost items, because by increasing the volume (thanks to low-cost sales), you will have the opportunity to earn higher payout percentages for high-end products.

Be sure to use different Amazon tracking IDs for different sites, so you can see which site is generating the most payments. Again you can see the importance of the 80/20 rule.

13. Create, Produce And Sell Your Product

If you feel very creative and a little inventor you could produce a product and sell it online keeping you 100% of the revenues. It requires a lot of attention at the beginning and carries a serious risk when compared to drop shipping.

But, it also offers much higher performance possibilities and, provided you have a warehouse to store the physical product. So start thinking about your specific tastes and what kind of product you might like to create.

Do not worry about production, there are a lot of ways to find quality producers online. Thanks to a thriving import scene, there is a huge online directory ecosystem that will help you find a manufacturer.

Here are some sites that you can use to get started: *Alibaba.com*

Alibaba is the world's largest directories of manufacturers and suppliers - a fact that has driven the company to $200 billion market capitalization. There are thousands of suppliers working with Alibaba with strong performance evaluations. Recommended as a platform for almost every product category.

GlobalSources.com

Global Sources - or GS – is Alibaba's closest competitor. There is no trade in guarantee, but you get a large evaluation and a lot of help with your order. Recommended if you can not find anything on Alibaba (highly unlikely).

Made-in-China.com

Made in China mainly deals with larger products and offers quality, inspection and reporting of the structures. Recommended especially for industrial products.

In addition to these three sites, there are also a number of LinkedIn groups you can contact to find a manufacturer for your industry.

14. Buy An Existing Online Business

Just invest a couple of thousand dollars and then you have a system that generates cash in your hands.

As with the purchase of any business, you will not necessarily have a hen from golden eggs within a year, but it will take some promotion work and you will be done.

Since the risk is higher and no passive income flow is ever safe, do not rush and do not believe every word you read online - Check daily visits in the months or in previous years.

Ok what do you think? Do you believe that any of these online businesses are for you? Do you think they will take too much time?

Here is a question that you have to answer honestly: How much time do you spend on television, leisure time, excessive laziness or other totally non-productive activities?

Try to take a pen and paper and count how many hours you throw away in a month.

Well, now try to think about how quickly your financial life could change if you start to dedicate even just one of those hours to grow an online business and increase your automatic revenue. Now that you have realized that, go get your financial freedom!

Chapter 6

2 Fundamental aspects to KEEP making passive income

Professional training As we have seen, passive income exisst, but not immediately. If I want to start a web marketing or network marketing activity, for example, I will begin to structure an action plan, which will take time to become automatic.

Unfortunately, however, people who start web marketing, think that after buying an ebook (which may be the best in the world), within 2 days will be the new rich internet gurus. It does not work like that and above all if you hope to find an ebook that with 4 clicks set for you an automatic entry you are out of the way.

Not even this ebook will make you rich, if you do not act upon what it teaches.

To be successful in all areas of life, we need a mixture of factors. You can have the best website in the world, but if you sell poor products inside, you will hardly be able to take advantage of the second rule of web marketing: customer loyalty. The first rule is your professional training.

A person who enters your site and finds valid information or valid products will tend not only to return, but also to propose it to other people. As a result, a disgruntled person will not only not return, but will talk badly about your site and the rumours run fast on the net.

But even assuming that you have the nicest site, with the most beautiful products and the lowest prices, it may not be enough, you have to know how to sell them. Maybe everything is perfect, but then you do not know enough to intrigue a user to buy it, he will go out and buy it somewhere else, even spending more.

With this I am not saying that it is impossible to become a web marketer, but we must consider it as a profession in every sense. If someone thinks of opening a good site and getting rich, without having the right skills, he has the wrong mindset, but if he dedicates the right time to his training, then he can really create a big source of cash flow.

Create partnerships

It is true, creating friendships, alliances and partnerships is fundamental. Having people working in your own field of interest near you can be very useful. You can exchange ideas, opinions and advice. On the other hand, if someone thinks, that this kind of alliances can be found between relatives and friends, he will find himself crashing into a wall. Friends and relatives, if not already in the sector, will be the biggest obstacle. They will be those who at every error will only put their finger in the wound, not because they do not love you, but because the brain rejects everything that does not understand. This is why I always suggest to work on your financial goals by your own and to share what you are doing only after getting the first sign of success. Remember that at the earlier stages your mindset is very weak and even the slightest critique can make it collapse.

Conclusion

T hank for making it through to the end of *Passive Income: 18 Strategies to Make 12,487$ a Month and Become Financially Free* , let's hope it was informative and able to provide you with all of the tools you need to achieve your financial goals The next step is to begin to apply what you have learned during the course of this book and get started right away. As you have understood, passive income cannot be obtained with a passive mentality. Getting "out there" is the first step to make anything happen and we suggest you to start as soon as possible.

We hope that you find these lessons valuable and that you got the information you were looking for. Creating a passive income lifestyle that works for you will give you an incredible feeling, especially at the beginning, when you make the first gains. We are thrilled for you to start and we cannot wait to see your results coming in. Finally, if you found this book useful in any way, a review on Amazon is always appreciated!